Welsh Narrow Gauge

Paul Plowman and Graham Plowman

Published by:

JPG-Publishing

Front Cover:
Double Fairlie No. 10 'Merddin Emrys' shunts
an additional coach onto its train at Portmadoc
on 10 July 1964.

This Page:
No.9 'Prince of Wales' is being coaled up
ready for a trip to Devils Bridge – 20 August
1965.

The track bed is now 'Riverside Terrace' and
the houses beyond the sheds on Greenfield
Street still exist. The bridge on the left of the
water tower is Heol-Y-Bont.

Rear Cover:
No.2 'Dolgoch' waits to depart from Towyn
Wharf with a train to Abergynolwyn.

Introduction and Dedication

Introduction

Our book "Welsh Narrow Gauge" draws exclusively on my largely unpublished collection of photographs, which have been collated and edited by my son Graham Plowman.

My collection covers the 20-year period from 1964 to 1984. We have included pictures of the three principal narrow gauge railways which were operating during the period. By 1984 the possibility of rebuilding the Welsh Highland Railway was still a dream and therefore not covered by our book.

The Vale of Rheidol Light Railway

The Vale of Rheidol Light Railway opened on 22nd December 1902 as a passenger railway between Aberystwyth and Devils Bridge, a distance of 10 miles, but also to serve the mines and logging along the Rheidol Valley. Using the Light Railways Act of 1896, authorisation from Parliament was obtained on 6th August 1897 for two sections of railway, its 'main' line to Devils Bridge and a ½ mile Harbour Branch.

Acquired by the Great Western Railway on 1st January 1922, the railway came under British Railways' control with Nationalisation on 1st January 1948. It remained as the last outpost of British Rail's steam operations and was eventually sold to the Brecon Mountain Railway in late 1989.

The Talyllyn Railway

The Talyllyn Railway open in December 1866 to transport slate from the quarries at Bryn Eglwys above Abergynowlwyn down to a wharf at Towyn for shipment by standard gauge railway, a distance of 7 miles. However, a passenger service to Abergynowlwyn was also operated from the outset. With 2ft-3in gauge already established in the Bryn Eglwys quarries, this was continued instead of the more usual 1ft-11½in narrow gauge 'standard'.

In 1911 joint control of the quarries and the railway passed to Sir Henry Hayden Jones who continued to operate a passenger service at a loss until his death in 1950. By then the railway was considerably run down with only one locomotive, 'Talyllyn' able to be steamed. Thanks to the generosity of Sir Henry Hayden Jones' executors ownership passed to the Talyllyn Railway Preservation Society in

1951, giving the railway the distinction of being the first statutory undertaking to be run by a preservation society – a World first.

Although Bryn Eglwys finally closed in 1947, the railway has since been extended to Nant Gwernol at the foot of the Bryn Eglwys inclines.

The Festiniog Railway

Today the Festiniog Railway operates between Portmadog and Blaenau Ffestiniog in North Wales, a distance of 13 miles. The line was first opened in 1836 as a horse-drawn tramway to bring slate from the quarries of Bleanau Ffestiniog to the port of Portmadoc to be shipped by sea.

Over the years tiles for roofing became more popular. However, by the outbreak of war in 1939 this traffic had all but ceased. A freight service continued until 1946. The railway lay derelict throughout the war years but never actually closed. On 22nd June 1954 the company was purchased by Allan Pegler and the Festiniog Railway Society registered as a company on 24th December 1954.

Since 1954 the Festiniog Railway has been progressively reopened and developed between Portmadoc and Blaenau Ffestiniog.

I made several trips to North Wales, commencing in 1964 with another in 1965. On both these trips I walked the Festiniog Railway from Bleanau Ffestiniog to Tan-y-Bwlch up past Moel Ystradau, following the route of the old railway. In 1969 I visited Ddault with my Wife, Irene, to see the progress made with construction of the Festiniog spiral. Finally, in 1984 I again undertook the walk from Bleanau Ffestiniog to Ddault this time following the line of the new railway in the company of my two elder children.

Dedications

I dedicate this book to my late Wife, Irene, for her enduring patience and support of my hobby, and to my three children, Graham, Christine and Jennifer who accompanied me on numerous walking and cycling trips.

Paul Plowman

July 2024

No.7 'Owain Glyndwr' in the loco shed at Aberystwyth. 20 August 1965

No.8 'Llywelyn' being coaled up in the loco depot at Aberystwyth. Today, this is the site of Riverside Terrace with the Afon Rheidol running parallel to the other side of the wall. 29 June 1964

No.9 'Prince of Wales' being coaled up in the loco depot at Aberystwyth.

In 1902, Davies and Metcalfe built two locomotives, No.1 'Edward VII' and No.2 'Prince of Wales', for the opening of the railway. When the Great Western took over in 1923, they were renumbered 1212 and 1213. Two new locomotives nos.7 and 8 were introduced, and No.1212 'Edward VII' and No.1213 'Prince of Wales' were withdrawn for overhauls. No.1213 was scrapped in 1923, and a new engine, identical to nos.7 and 8, was introduced as a heavily overhauled no.1213. This new engine was renumbered No.9 by British Railways in 1948.

No.9 *'Prince of Wales'* being coaled up in the loco depot at Aberystwyth. The track to the left was all that remained of the Harbour Branch. 20 August 1965

No.9 '*Prince of Wales*' being coaled up in the loco depot at Aberystwyth on 20 August 1965.

No.8 'Llywelyn' being backed into Aberystwyth Station on 29 June 1964.

No.8 'Llywelyn' was built in 1923 at the Great Western Railway's Swindon works, along with no.7 to replace earlier locomotives No.1 "Edward VII" and No.2 "Prince of Wales".

No.8 *'Llywelyn'* being backed into Aberystwyth Station on 29 June 1964.

Originally built with vacuum braking and steam heating, the front buffer beam displays a hole and bracket to the left of the coupling where the steam heating pipe was once fitted.

No.9 *'Prince of Wales'* shunting stock at Aberystwyth on 20 August 1965.

All three Vale of Rheidol railway locomotives were originally known by their numbers. They were named in 1955/56 under British Railways' ownership.

No.8 'Llywelyn' shunts an additional coach onto the train of the day at Aberystwyth. 29 June 1964

No.9 'Prince of Wales' at Aberystwyth ready to depart for Devils Bridge on 19 August 1965.

No.9 ‘*Prince of Wales*’ at Aberystwyth ready to depart for Devils Bridge.

The canopies of the GWR terminus can be seen in the background. 20 August 1965

No.8 *'Llywelyn'* departs from Aberystwyth, crossing Park Avenue, with the train of the day on 29 June 1964.

19 August 1965 and a Hillman Super-Minx waits on Park Avenue while No.7 'Owain Glyndwr' crosses on its departure from Aberystwyth to Devils Bridge.

78xx Manor Class 4-6-0 No. 7802 '*Bradley Manor*' passing the Vale of Rheidol exchange sidings with a goods train to Aberystwyth on 19 August 1965.

This locomotive is now preserved on the Severn Valley Railway.

No.9 'Prince of Wales' crossing the original Afon Rheidol bridge at Llanbadarnfawr on 18 August 1965.

The British Railways' main line to Shrewsbury via Dovey junction and Machynlleth can be seen in the background.

No.8 'Llywelyn' running alongside the Afon Rheidol passes Glanrafon Halt on 18 August 1965.

No.8 'Llywelyn' starts the long climb at Capel Bangor on 18 August 1965.

The final four mile climb to Devils Bridge is a continuous gradient of 1 in 50. No.7 'Owain Glyndwr' takes water at Aberffrwd. The loop is clipped out of use and water is being taken from the adjacent water crane. 17 August 1965

Water tower at Aberffrwd Station with ground frame adjacent. 30 June 1964.

This water tower still exists but the tank is no longer painted decoratively.

Ground frame at Aberffrwd Station on 30 June 1964.

Aberffrwd Station with the passing loop clipped out of use and signal arms removed. 30 June 1964

On 19 August 1965, a view from the train showing the numerous sharp curves on the final section to Devils Bridge.

Devils Bridge viewed from Ystumtuen on 17 August 1965. The route of the railway can be seen skirting the tops of the hills across the valley opposite.

The approach to Devils Bridge, with the station behind the camera, looking towards Aberystwyth on 1 July 1964.

The Water tower at Devils Bridge. The detail shown here makes it an ideal candidate for modellers. 17 August 1965

No.8 'Llywelyn' approaching Devils Bridge with a train from Aberystwyth on 17 August 1965.

Left: View of Devils Bridge Station. 1 July 1964

Above: Devils Bridge Station building at the end of the line. 1 July 1964

The station building at Devils Bridge. 1 July 1964

The starter signal and over bridge at Devils Bridge Station. 1 July 1964

No.7 'Owain Glyndwr' arrives at Devils Bridge with a train from Aberystwyth on 17 August 1965.

No.9 *Prince of Wales* is run round its train at Devils Bridge on 17 August 1984.

No.9 'Prince of Wales' is filled with water at Devils Bridge. By this time the locomotive had been converted to oil burning. The water tower is looking somewhat neglected when compared with its full GWR colour scheme on page 28. 17 August 1984

No.9 *'Prince of Wales'* about to draw forward to shunt its train into the departure platform at Devils Bridge on 17 August 1984.

No.9 'Prince of Wales' about to draw forward to shunt its train into the departure platform at Devils Bridge on 17 August 1984.

Motion of No.7 'Owain Glyndwr' as it waits to depart from Devils Bridge on 17 August 1965.

No.9 *Prince of Wales* waits to depart from Devils Bridge on 1 July 1964.

The locomotive is seen here in a 'BR lined loco green' livery with post–1956 crest, complete with GWR style copper capped chimney and valve cover.

The Vale of Rheidol, a view now hidden by forestry. 1 July 1964

No.9 'Prince of Wales' descends from Devils Bridge on 1 July 1964.

No.9 'Prince of Wales' is run round its train on arrival at Aberystwyth on 1 July 1964.

At this time, the Vale of Rheidol terminus was outside the former GWR terminus, the wall of which can be seen on the right. In 1968, the VoR terminus was relocated to the other side of this wall as can be seen in the following pages.

In 1964, the former standard gauge Carmarthen line platforms at Aberystwyth were closed. This provided the opportunity for Vale of Rheidol trains to access the main line station and it was no longer necessary to loop around under the Carmarthen line. In 1968, the VoR terminus was moved into the former standard gauge platforms and the line re-routed. Here we see No.9 'Prince of Wales' about to be run round its train at Aberystwyth on 17 August 1984.

A crossover was installed to enable locomotives to be run round trains and depart to the engine shed for servicing. Here we see No 9 'Prince of Wales' in 'Cambrian Railways' livery with its number now painted on the buffer beam instead of the smokebox door, being run round its train on 17 August 1984.

The 'new' 1968 terminus of the VoR at Aberystwyth, located between the former Carmarthen line platforms. The Carmarthen line curved away to the right behind the train and beyond the white building. In the left background, the former GWR engine shed is being used by the VoR. To the right of the engine shed is the former GWR brick-built coaling stage with a 45,000 gallon water tank. It was built circa 1925 as part of the re-modelling of the locomotive depot at Aberystwyth Station. By 1996 it had been demolished, to provide extra parking spaces for the adjacent car park, leaving the tower at Didcot as the only ex-GWR type still standing in Britain. 17 August 1984

The Talyllyn Railway

No.1 'Talyllyn' outside Towyn Pendre's carriage shed. The locomotive was available for service, although not in steam as evidenced by the cap on its chimney (to prevent rain ingress into the smokebox). 4 July 1964

Left and above: No.1 'Talyllyn' outside the carriage shed at Towyn Pendre works on 4 July 1964.

Above and right: No.2 'Dolgoch' simmers at Towyn Pendre engine shed ready to haul the train of the day to Abergynolwyn. 4 July 1964

New in April 1952, Machynlleth–allocated BR Standard Class 3 2-6-2T No. 82000 passes the Talyllyn Wharf at Towyn with a train to Pwllheli on 4 July 1964. Note the GWR lower-quadrant signal which stands in-line with the Tallylyn Railway station.

Against the backdrop of a pair of magnificent Victorian semi–detached villas overlooking the sea, No.2 'Dolgoch' waits to depart from Towyn Wharf with a train to Abergynolwyn on 4 July 1964. A similar 1984 view can be seen on the following page.

Towyn Wharf Station with No.6 'Douglas' in the background. 16th August 1984. Since 1964 the track-layout has been simplified and much new housing has been built. A Plasser track machine sits in British Rail's Wharf siding.

No.6 'Douglas' at Towyn Wharf on 16 August 1984. The picture on page 52 was taken from British Rail's over bridge on the right of this picture (Neptune Road).

Left and above: With a pre-1959 Bedford CA peeking out from behind the station building, No.2 'Dolgoch' waits to depart from Towyn Wharf with a train to Abergynolwyn on 4 July 1964.

No.2 'Dolgoch' awaits its crew prior to departure from Towyn Wharf on 4 July 1964.

The former Corris Railway coach at Towyn Wharf on 4 July 1964. Built in 1898 by Metropolitan Railway Carriage and Wagon Co. Ltd in Saltley, Birmingham, this coach was one of the last two coaches built for the Corris Railway and is the only surviving coach still in use. Following withdrawal of passenger services on the Corris Railway in 1930, coaches No.7 and 8 were sold for greenhouse/chicken coup use. In 1959, No.8 was purchased by the Talyllyn Railway from a garden in Gobowen, moved to the works at Pendre and fully restored on a new underframe. It entered service in 1961 as Talyllyn Railway No.17. By 2018, major bodywork repairs and rebuilding were required and it is now back in service.

A further view of No.2 'Dolgoch' waiting to depart from Towyn Wharf with a train to Abergynolwyn.
4 July 1964

No.4 'Sir Hayden' passes Towyn Pendre with a train to Nant Gwernol on 16 August 1984. Note the distinctive tumblehome on the first coach (a three-compartment four-wheeled vehicle).

As railway staff close the level crossing gates, No.4 'Sir Hayden' disappears into the distance from Towyn Pendre on its way to Nant Gwernol. 16 August 1984

No.1 'Talyllyn' commences its run round at Abergynolwyn on 3 July 1964.

Above and right: No.1 'Talyllyn' running round at Abergynolwyn on 3 July 1964. The young lad looking on could well be in retirement now!

Above and left: No.1. '*Talyllyn*' is prepared for its departure from Abergynolwyn on 3 July 1964.

No.1 'Talyllyn' departs from Abergynolwyn with its train to Towyn on 3 July 1964.

At Nant Gwernol No.6 '*Douglas*' runs round its train on 16 August 1984.

Above and right: No.6 'Douglas' passes Towyn Pendre carriage shed with a train from Nant Gwernol on 16 August 1984.

The locomotive sheds and workshops in the relatively restricted depot site at Towyn Pendre on 16 August 1984.

The Festiniog Railway

'*Linda*' arrives at Minffordd with a train to Tan-y-bwlch on 6 July 1964.

Built by the Hunslet Engine Company, Leeds in 1893 as an 0-4-0 for the Penrhyn Quarry Railway, '*Linda*' moved to the Festiniog Railway on 14 July 1962 and was steamed the next day. Initially on hire, she was purchased in December 1963 for £1000, fitted with superheating in 1969 and in 1970, was rebuilt as a 2-4-0 Saddle Tank Tender (STT) engine using a pair of wheels from the rear bogie of long-since scrapped '*Moel Tryfan*'. In October 1970, '*Linda*' was converted to oil firing. She is seen here with the tender from '*Welsh Pony*' which was rebuilt and widened.

Above and left: 'Linda' is run round its train at Tan-y-bwlch. At this time (6 July 1964), Tan-y-bwlch was the limit of passenger services.

As built, 'Linda' did not have train brakes. She is seen here, still in 0-4-0 form and with vacuum brakes fitted.

Above and right: On 6 July 1964 '*Linda*' departs from Tan-y-bwlch with a train to Portmadoc.

Double Fairlie No.10 'Merddin Emrys' approaches Tan-y-bwlch through the woods near Whistling Curve with a train from Portmadoc on 6 July 1964.

No.10 'Merddin Emrys' was the first locomotive constructed by the Festiniog Railway Company at its Boston Lodge workshops and was the third Double Fairlie locomotive built for the railway. Designed by George Percival Spooner and completed in 1879, Merddin Emrys has spent its entire operational life on the Festiniog Railway. When the railway ceased operations in 1946, 'Merddin Emrys' was the only Double Fairlie engine remaining in service.

Double Fairlie No.10 'Merddin Emrys' at Tan-y-bwlch. 6 July 1964.

In its early years of preservation, 'Merddin Emrys' ran without a cab roof.

Double Fairlie No.10 'Merddin Emrys' at Tan-y-bwlch on 6 July 1964.

No.10 'Merddin Emrys' departs from Tan-y-bwlch with a train to Portmadoc on 6 July 1964.

No.2 'Prince' arrives at Pen Cob having been released from a returning train at Portmadoc on 10 July 1964.

Originally named 'The Prince' (prior to 1892), this locomotive is one of the original Festiniog Railway engines. Over its lifetime, it underwent several rebuilds. When the FR ceased operating in 1946, it was left in the works with its overhaul unfinished. However, when the railway reopened on 23 July 1965, it became the first of the rebuilt locomotives to be put back into service.

With Austin A30 and Ford vans on the causeway, No.10 'Merddin Emrys' approaches Portmadoc, running light from Boston Lodge works on 10 July 1964.

The single 'F' spelling of Festiniog is contained within the Festiniog Railway Act of 1832 that enabled the railway.

Above and left: No.10 'Merddin Emrys' is prepared at Portmadoc on 10 July 1964 for a return trip to Tan-y-bwlch.

No.10 'Merddin Emrys' sets back onto its train at Portmadoc on 10 July 1964.

No.10 'Merddin Emrys' picks up an additional coach to shunt across onto its train at Portmadoc on 10 July 1964.

Above and right: No.10 'Merddin Emrys' shunts an additional coach on to its train at Portmadoc on 10 July 1964.

Finally, the fireman makes his last checks as No.10 'Merddin Emrys' waits to depart from Portmadoc with the train to Tan-y-bwlch. 10 July 1964

'Blanche' arrives at Portmadoc from Boston Lodge ready to take a train to Tan-y-bwlch on 10 July 1964 (photograph shows its cab prior to reprofiling in 1965).

'Blanche' arrived on the Festiniog Railway on 17 December 1963 and is seen here in close to original condition as an 0-4-0, but having had vacuum brakes fitted and a temporary tender attached. The tender had been used by 'Linda' but originated from 'Palmerston'. Converted to oil firing in April 1971, and rebuilt as a 2-4-0 later that year, she acquired the other spare pair of wheels from the rear bogie of scrapped 'Moel Tryfan'.

No.10 'Merddin Emrys' returns from Tan-y-bwlch with its train to Portmadoc. 10 July 1964

No.10 'Merddin Emrys' departs to Boston Lodge works while 'Blanche' removes a coach from the train in the background. 10 July 1964

'*Blanche*' shunts back the coach from a train at Portmadoc. 10 July 1964

Shunting completed, 'Blanche' waits to depart from Portmadoc with a train to Tan-y-bwlch on 10 July 1964.

Above and left: 'Blanche' finally departs from Portmadoc with its train to Tan-y-bwlch on 10 July 1964.

Site of former Duffws Station at Bleanau Ffestiniog. The bridge from which this picture was taken has been removed and the High Street levelled. In this 22 August 1965 view an Austin J2 van, Ford Thames (307E Anglia) van and a Hillman Minx saloon can also be seen.

Former LNWR exchange yard at Bleanau Ffestiniog. 22 August 1965

Above and right: Site of former Festiniog Railway station opposite the LNWR station (right of picture) at Bleanau Ffestiniog. 22 August 1965

Site of former Festiniog Railway station opposite the LNWR station (left of picture) at Bleanau Ffestiniog.
22 August 1965

Glanypwll Road Level Crossing (towards Portmadoc) with an MG Magnette parked in the driveway to its left on 22 August 1965. These houses are still in place.

Bridge over the Afon Barlwyd looking towards Bleanau Ffestiniog. Note the tapered sleepers providing 'cant'.
22 August 1965

North at Barlwyd Terrace (left) on the outskirts on Tan-y-grisiau. 22 August 1965

Near Pant Y Celyn, Tan-y-grisiau (towards Bleanau Ffestiniog). 22 August 1965

Near Pant Y Celyn, Tan-y-grisiau (towards Bleanau Ffestiniog). 22 August 1965

The site of the former Ffestiniog Railway station at Tan-y-grisiau (towards Bleanau Ffestiniog). Many of the buildings in this picture are still standing today. South from Tan-y-grisiau station all the the way to the Moelwyn Tunnel, the track had been removed and the area flooded by Lyn Ystradau, the lower reservoir of the CEGB pumped storage scheme. 22 August 1965

A Morris Minor parked on the site of the former Festiniog Railway station at Tan-y-grisiau. Up to this location (from behind the photographer) the track had been removed and the route flooded by the lower reservoir of the CEGB pumped storage scheme. 22 August 1965

North-end portal of the abandoned Moelwyn Tunnel. 22 August 1965

South-end portal of the abandoned Moelwyn Tunnel. 22 August 1965

New embankment under construction for the Deviation at Ddault. 22 August 1965

New cutting under construction for the Deviation at Ddault. 22 August 1965

Future site of the new Ddault Station. 22 August 1965.

The line is seen here in its original layout and continued straight to the old Moelwyn Tunnel. The new deviation would commence with a curve to the right just before the bushes in the far distance.

'*Linda*' driven by General Manager, Allan Garraway, waits to leave Tan-y-bwlch with a train to Portmadoc on 22 August 1965.

'*Linda*' departs from Tan-y-bwlch with a train to Portmadoc on 22 August 1965.

No.11 *Earl of Merioneth* is run around at Ddault. 4 June 1969

The new Rhoslyn Bridge and embankments under construction at Ddault. 4 June 1969

The new Rhoslyn Bridge and embankments under construction at Ddault. 4 June 1969

'*Blanche*' is run round its train at Ddault on 4 June 1969.

By this time, the rear of the original cab had been removed and a new cab added to the tender to provide protection for crews. The loco was converted to a 2-4-0 in 1971/72.

'*Blanche*' departs from Tan-y-bwlch with a train to Portmadoc on 4 June 1969.

No.11 'Earl of Merioneth' arrives at Tan-y-bwlch with a train to Ddault on 4 June 1969.

'Earl of Merioneth' was the second locomotive to be built by the FR at Boston Lodge and the fourth FR Double Fairlie. Two years after this picture, it was deemed uneconomical to repair due to years of work and was withdrawn. It was then cosmetically restored as No.3 with its original name 'Livingston Thomson' and displayed at the National Railway Museum at York. A new replacement No.11 'Earl of Merioneth' was built and can be seen later in this book.

No.11 'Earl of Merioneth' departs from Tan-y-bwlch with a train to Ddault on 4 June 1969.

14 August 1984 and the replacement Bleanau Ffestiniog terminus of the Festiniog Railway is on the left of the picture. The standard gauge tracks on the right are for the replacement terminus of the former LNWR branch from Llandudno Junction which had opened on 22 March 1982.

25 May 1982 saw the opening of Bleanau Ffestiniog's replacement terminus for the Festiniog Railway (photographed here on 14 August 1984).

Bleanau Ffestiniog looking southwards. British Rail's branch to Llandudno Junction curves away to the right. 14 August 1984

'*Moelwyn*' departs from Bleanau Ffestiniog terminus with a train to Portmadog on 14 August 1984; 'Portmadoc' having been changed to 'Porthmadog' in 1974. *A Renault 4 van and the rear of a (rare) Ford Mk4 Zephyr Estate in the adjacent yard also date the photograph.*

Looking towards Portmadog and now a wooded area to the left of the track, this was the site of the former Festiniog Railway station at Bleanau Ffestiniog, in turn located opposite the LNWR station (right of picture on the far side of North Western Road) on 14 August 1984. *Compare this with the same view on page 100.*

Looking back towards Bleanau Ffestiniog station, the site of the former Festiniog Railway station with the former LNWR station (out of left of picture) on 14 August 1984. *Compare this with the same view on page 101. The same stepped wall on the left of the road can be seen in both pictures.*

Glanypwll Road Level Crossing on 14 August 1984. *Compare this with the same view on page 103.*

No.3 '*Mountaineer*' approaches Blaenau Ffestiniog with a train from Portmadog on 14 August 1984.

No.3 'Mountaineer' approaches Tan–y–grisiau Station with a train to Portmadog on 14 August 1984.

No.11 'Earl of Merioneth' crosses the new level crossing south of Tan-y-grisiau with a train to Portmadog on 14 August 1984.

This was one of two new level crossings across public highways (there is a third vehicular accommodation crossing at Tan-y-grisiau station) necessary for re-establishment of the railway line between Tan-y-grisiau and Ddault.

The new No.11 'Earl of Merioneth' continues south from Tan-y-grisiau with its train to Portmadog on 14 August 1984.

This locomotive replaced the original 'Earl of Merioneth' which is now at the National Railway Museum, York and has reverted to its original name 'Livingston Thomson' (No.3). The new locomotive is seen here and was completed in 1979. Subsequent modifications have seen its 'square' appearance changed to a more traditional FR-style loco. It was withdrawn in 2018 in need of major work and remains out of service.

No.10 'Merddin Emrys' approaches Tan-y-grisiau behind the power station with a train from Portmadog. In the event of a derailment, the external guard rails would assist in protecting the buried water pipes (from the high dam), which pass under the railway. 14 August 1984

'*Blanche*' emerges from the northern portal of the new Moelwyn Tunnel on 14 August 1984.

Southern portal of the old Moelwyn Tunnel on 14 August 1984. Very little has changed in almost twenty years since the photograph on page 111 was taken.

Approach to the south-end portal of the old Moelwyn Tunnel. 14 August 1984

Abandoned track bed and footbridge near Ddault. Today, only the approaches either side to this bridge exist in a partially demolished state. 14 August 1984

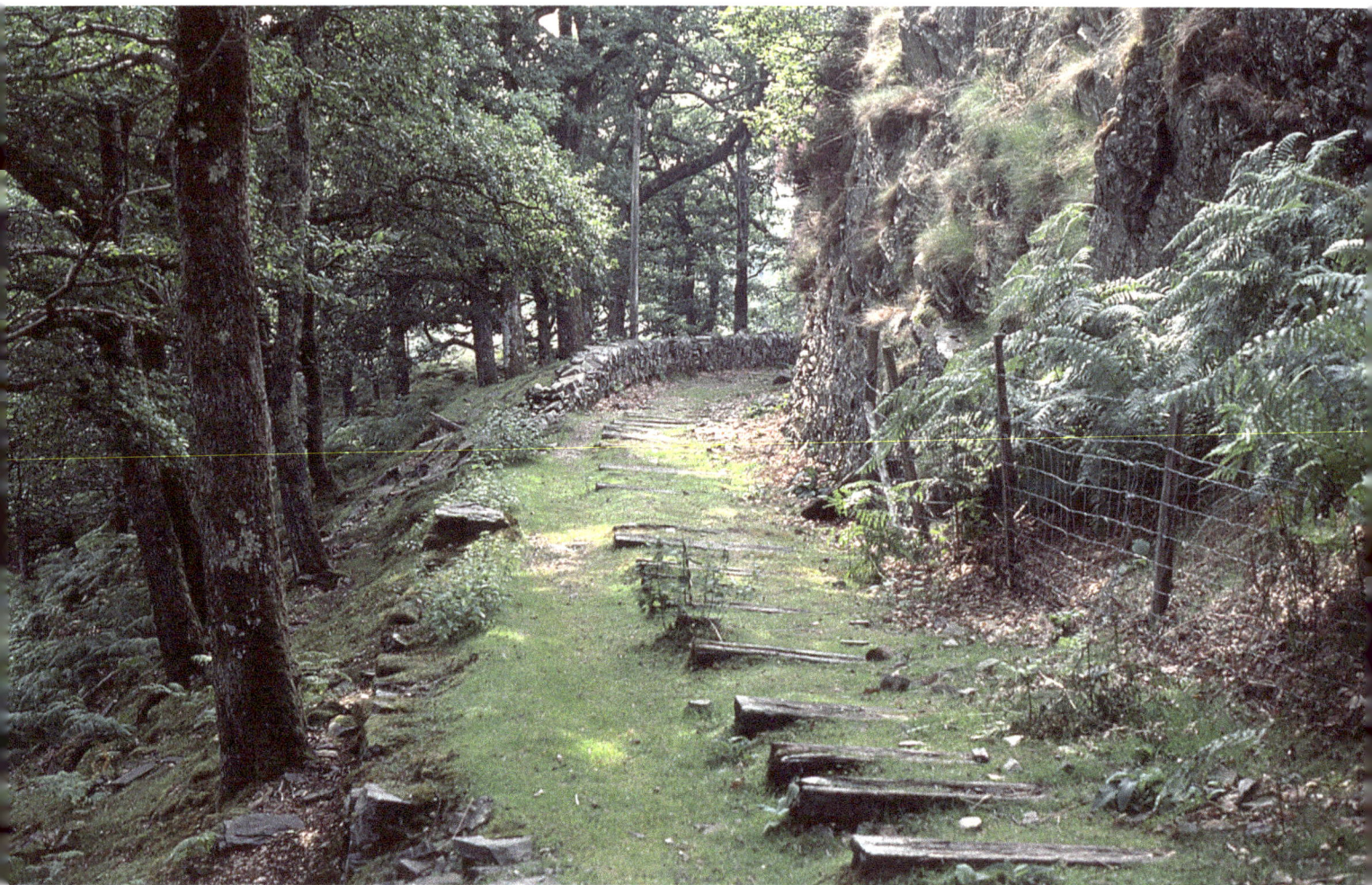

Abandoned track bed near Ddault. 14 August 1984

No.3 'Mountaineer' enters the Deviation as it departs from Ddault with a train to Blaneau Ffestiniog on 14 August 1984.

The embankment in the distance on the right of this picture is the former track bed to the old Moelwyn tunnel.

New No.11 'Earl of Merioneth' and No.3 'Mountaineer' pass at Ddault on 14 August 1984.

New No.11 'Earl of Merioneth' passes the stone marking the location of commencement of work on the Deviation. The stone is to be seen in the far left of the picture. 14 August 1984

Other Titles from JPG-Publishing

◄ Last of Southern Steam

A collection of photos of the Last of Southern Steam, including Waterloo, Nine Elms, Basingstoke, The North Downs line, Swanage and Lymington.

ISBN: 978-1-7637924-1-8

Severn Valley Railway ►

A collection of photos of the Severn Valley Railway.

ISBN: 978-1-7637924-2-5

◄ West Somerset Railway

A collection of photos of the West Somerset Railway between 2004 and 2007.

ISBN: 978-1-7637924-3-2

www.jpg-publishing.com

www.ingramcontent.com/pod-product-compliance
Lightning Source LLC
Chambersburg PA
CBHW061226150426
42812CB00054BA/2533

* 9 7 8 1 7 6 3 7 9 2 4 0 1 *